BLUE AND THE SPANISH MUSTANG HORSE STORIES

LOON LAKE RANCH, MONTANA

by Phyllis Falconer

Loon Lake (foreground) and Ranch meadows (background)

Sundown   Quanah
Dudley Slough

TABLE OF CONTENTS

Fork In the Road

← *1 mile to Dudley Slough*   *1 mile to Loon Lake* →

Main Gate to Loon Lake Ranch

Loon Lake

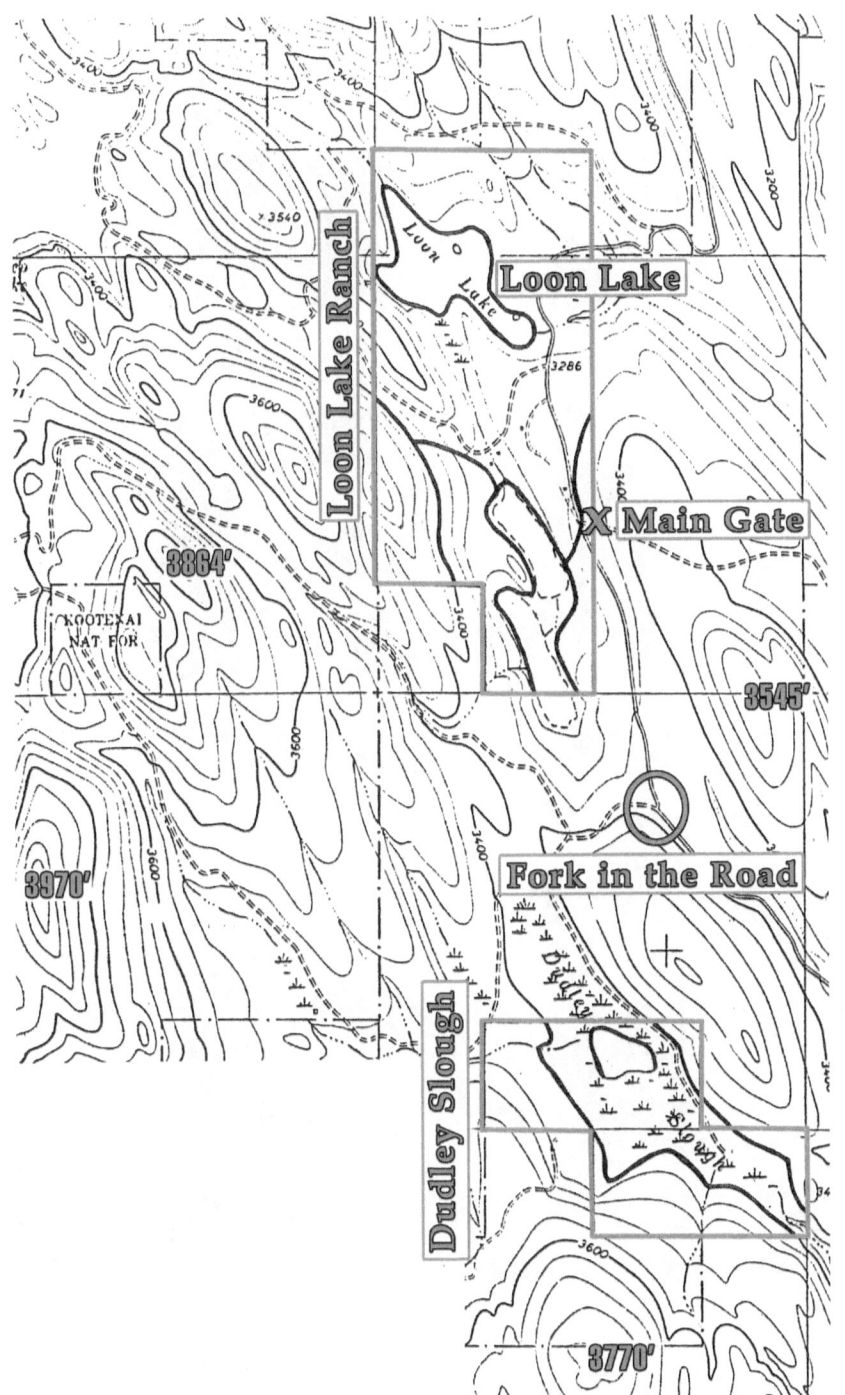

Ranch House

Geldings, Jacques, and Mam

Front Acre and Hayfield

PROLOGUE

Loon Lake Ranch and the Spanish Mustangs formed my life from 1969 to 1992. These stories were written the winter of 1992 while still clear in my mind, then packed away.

The stories and accompanying photographs were unpacked eighteen years later after a chance attendance at a local Writers Group. After a great deal of encouragement, the original stories are now published.

Mares at Dudley Slough

BLUE

June 1969

City bred and reared, I was totally green to ranching and mountain living, and had only a few months of riding lessons. We, my husband who would leave at the end of summer for his out-of- state job, and our two sons, who would be going off to college, parked the travel trailer in a Montana meadow, our home while a small house was being built nearby.

1920. Bob Brislawn and his Spanish Mustang Pack String

Excited to start my new life, I had to have a horse now, and it had to be a Spanish Mustang . Reading about old Bob Brislawn and his efforts to save the descendents of the horses the Spanish Conquistadores rode, fired my desire to help. Brislawn, a packer for the Geological Survey for thirty years, relied on these tough, intelligent, attractive horses as the western United States was being mapped. Now in retirement on his ranch in Wyoming, he knew only a few small bands, still carrying the genes and conformation of the Spanish horse, survived in remote mountainous regions and realized, "they best be saved." Bob, along with a few other concerned, and knowledgeable breeders, has saved the Spanish Mustang from oblivion.

Azul (Blue) a two year old grulla stallion, as well as the owner's hand-made, open top, one-horse trailer were available near Tucson, Arizona, and that is where I headed in July. After a brief initiation to Blue and a few practice loadings into the little trailer with a manger and wind screen in the front, but no escape door, we were on the road. I was given strict instructions to unload and walk Blue around at least every four hours and to find a good place for him at night.

Blue and I had one thing in common: inexperience. He was dutifully unloaded at rest stops, watered, and walked around. I would lead him up to the trailer and say, "Get in Blue" and he would walk in. Amazing, because over the years, I have had to deal with all kinds of balky, uncooperative

Blue, 2 years, Arizona

horses, and know how exasperating it is to try to load an unwilling horse. If Blue had not walked into the trailer, I would not have known what to do. At night, I would find him a corral, either private, or in a public fairgrounds where he could exercise and move around. In the morning he was glad to see me, and always walked in the trailer for his horse pellets.

And so my years with Blue began; years of mutual respect and cooperation. He was my first horse and the first horse I ever trained.

YANA

August 1969

Yana, a two year old blue roan filly had just been
trailered home from the Brislawn's Cayuse Ranch, and
had been introduced to Blue in the small acre pasture.

She loved the Montana
grass and soon
developed a very round
belly for such a little
thing. She lay down to
take a nap,
unfortunately choosing
a depression in the
ground. When she tried
to get up, her legs
sprawled uphill and her

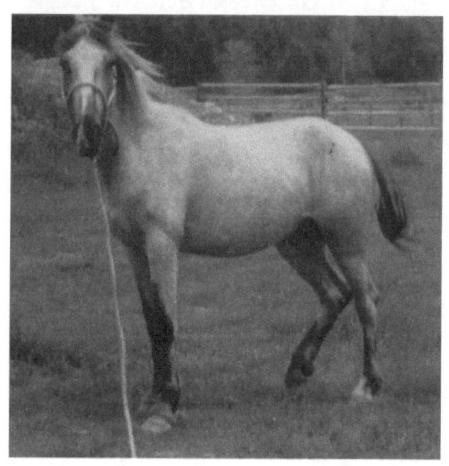

Yana

round belly prevented her from rolling over to use her
legs on the downhill side of the shallow hole. Her
thrashing made Blue nervous and he circled her.
Suddenly he knelt down by her head, grasped her neck
skin in his teeth and attempted to pull her out. Again
and again he tried to pull her up while we ran toward
them. We soon had ropes on her feet and flipped her
over. Tired and exhausted, Yana was okay. For us, there

4

was a growing respect for Blue, the young stallion, and the ways of the Spanish Mustang.

CHIPPER

September 1969

As Emmett eased the big barn door open, Chipper a five-year old stallion that now belonged to me, charged out snorting. Not wasting anytime looking around or choosing a better way, he galloped across the corral, crashed through the fence breaking the wooden boards, and raced down the pasture to join the other horses.

Was this the same gentle, rideable Chip intended as a saddle horse, I admired in his pasture in North Dakota a few months ago? He had been recently trailered to the

Cayuse Ranch in Wyoming for me to pick up and it was too late to back out now.

Chip was eventually caught and loaded into my little one-horse trailer. Stopping for the night at the Butte, Montana fairgrounds, I backed the trailer up to an empty stall, blocking the door, with Chip inside munching hay. My sleeping bag was spread out in the stall next to his, and with a full stomach, he was quiet all night. Not wanting this powerhouse charging through my fences, I pulled into a small town fifty miles from home, where Chip was gelded and cared for while he healed.

Gentler now but still powerful, Chip was corralled that winter with Tonka behind the house. A wooden feeder had been attached to the far wall of his stall. Chip had his nose deep in the trough when a large chunk of snow on the roof slid off landing in a heap just outside the stall. Chip did not wait to raise his head out of the feeder. He spun around ripping the feeder off the wall and raced out, hitting and knocking the big metal gate in the corral off its hinges and running over it. The next time snow fell off the roof, he kindly jumped the gate.

Having more enthusiasm than experience in those early days on the ranch, I was eager to try out Chip on the cutter I had just acquired. He was being cooperative as a saddle horse, riding around the ranch on snow-covered trails, so I thought he was ready to pull the cutter. After a few times of teaching him to back into the shafts and buckling on the harness, we were ready to go, even though I knew I should have spent more time teaching him to pull a lighter load. Oh, well, let's give it a try.

I climbed into the cutter, picked up the reins, and asked Chip to move out. The sound of the runners on the snow and the unaccustomed weight was more than he could

tolerate. Off we lurched at a wild gallop. Stopping him was impossible. We charged through the pasture gate, which was fortunately open, the end of the cutter hanging up on the gate post, but Chip kept going breaking his traces. Free now from the monster behind, he galloped around in the snow, otherwise we would still be flying along in the cutter, heaven knows where.

TONKA

April 1970

The first spring after I brought Tonka, a nine year old gelding, to the ranch and still fairly green to riding, we took off for a little spin. The snow was gone, but in the dark woods where the sun did not reach, a huge frozen puddle filled the dirt road, from side to side, about thirty feet long. Tonka walked carefully along the narrow bit of bank between ice and thick trees. After trotting and walking a few miles, then turning around to come home, smart Tonka pulled one of his many tricks on me. He suddenly dropped his head getting a long reach of rein,

 stuck out his nose and neck, and leaped into a fast gallop. Not knowing how to bend his nose down to engage the reins and knowing what was up ahead waiting for us, I crouched down deep in the saddle. Flying along, Tonka was having great fun as we careened toward the ice. He hit it dead center, lost his footing, dropped to his knees, and slid along the length of the ice, coming to a stop at the edge. He stood up but I

9

had him now, and we walked sedately home.

Every subsequent year, Tonka had his spring run, the
only time of the year he wanted to run. On a day of his
choosing, he would get jiggly and excited. Riding at a
rather fast walk, we headed for a suitable place, usually
"Tonka's Hill." "O.K. Tonka, let's go!," and off he
charged, knowing he could run as fast and as far as he
wanted. Then, for the rest of the year, he was dependable
Tonka, safe for anyone to ride.

CHIPPER

May 1970

Chip and Tonka, the two saddle horses, were pastured in the barn field at Dudley Slough, which extended to the east boundary fence. Wanting to check that fence and gate, I jumped on Chip with just a halter and lead line on him and rode the quarter mile or so to the fence. As I turned him to walk back, he suddenly leaped into a gallop and we tore down the trail through the woods with me clinging to his mane. We were going so fast my eyes watered and I had trouble breathing. Curiously, as Chip's speed increased, his body flattened out. Tail, back, neck, and head seemed to be level. The more he flattened, the smoother the ride, no bounce. We flashed across the meadow with Chip executing a beautiful sliding stop in front of the old barn and Tonka.

Later, I cleared rocks and twigs from a quarter mile of flat trail, thinking to duplicate his speed with proper saddle and bridle for control, stop watch in hand. No matter how many times I encouraged him to gallop flat out, we never again achieved that breathless bareback speed.

BECKY

June 1972

Good heavens - a glance in the rear view mirror of the old Dodge pickup showed Becky, my tan and brown Toggenberg milk goat, racing down the road, her udder whipping back and forth. I stopped the truck, leaped out, dropped the tail gate, and Becky jumped in.

Becky, colt, Yana

She had just been left at the farm where I had acquired her, sometime previously, and thought she would feel at home there while she came into heat and was bred. Goats are tricky to breed, as they only come into heat for one day, and will only accept a billy within a few hours. It is necessary to breed them once a year to keep their milk flowing, and flow she did, three quarts a day, which fed the chickens, two dogs, a cat and all the milk, cheese and yogurt I could use.

She obviously no longer considered her birthplace tolerable. She wanted to go back to her home where she thought she was a human like me, or a dog when she was with friendly Jacques and Tammy. Even the horses tolerated her when she invaded their space. At first, I tried to keep her penned, but she would have none of that - climbing up and over the wire enclosure or digging under. I let her loose, and she did not stray far from the house.

The next day, I drove back to the goat farm to bring home a smelly, aggressive billy. I chose a small one, hoping Becky would keep him under control. She did, eventually coming into heat, allowing herself to be bred and I could finally take the obnoxious billy home to his farm.

Sometimes Becky was a nuisance, eating the tops of anything planted. If I chastised her, she would angrily sink her horns into a hay bale and rip it to pieces. In the winter, if I wanted to use my cross-country skies to check on pastures, she would step on the backs of my skies, wanting to go along for the ride,

Becky and the billy on visitors' car

not wanting to be left behind, because she knew if the dogs went with me, she would be shut up in the barn. She could not go far in the snow, as her small feet would sink in and it was too tiring for her.

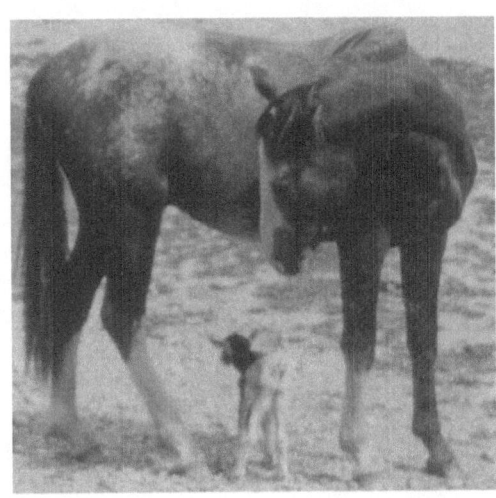

Young colt and Becky's kid

Whenever Becky, Jacques and Tammy heard a car or truck approaching, they would be at the front driveway, waiting to check out the newcomers. One time it was the insurance agent who needed to take a picture of the house for his files. It had rained the day before, leaving the ground a little wet. As I was walking toward the agent, Becky suddenly rose up on her hind legs and planted two muddy hooves on the front of his crisply ironed white shirt. O dear, she had never done that before!

Another time, busy in the front acre, I happened to look up, and Becky was staring out the upstairs window of the house. She had never walked up the stairs before, either, or pushed open a door. Becky, for all her antics, enlivened Loon Lake Ranch, and was friendly with everyone except the insurance agent.

TONKA

August 1972

Glacier National Park - fantastically beautiful with it's high mountains, cold glacier lakes and streams, forests and alpine meadows, mountain goat, moose and grizzly bear. My friend, Lydia, and I planned to hike with backpacks on sixty miles of trails that extend across the

northern end of the park, going over three passes. Our packs were unwieldy and heavy and minutes before driving away from the ranch, we decided to take Tonka. I doubted if he had ever been a pack horse, and I had never packed a horse.

*Hole in the Wall
Glacier Park*

Before we had even walked a quarter mile of trail, the old Calvary saddle with all our gear tied to it, listed heavily to port and sank under his belly. Tonka stopped in his tracks, and I knew I had a good pack horse. Trial and error, and many miles later, the saddle and load stayed topside.

Arriving at the Belly River ranger station late afternoon, we stopped to ask if we could put Tonka in their empty corral for the night. He took one look at Tonka with stuff tied all over him and burst out laughing, while Tonka and his embarrassed handler suffered through this indignity. He did let Tonka stay in the corral and pointed to a place down the hill along the river where we could camp. Next to the camp area stood a large tree with boards nailed on for toe holds if needed for a quick climb. Lydia said, "This certainly is griz country." We pitched our tent close to the tree.

After dark, we heard loud crashing in the woods coming nearer and nearer. Griz! I grabbed the flashlight and shined it over the top of the small tent and picked out two big, red eyes shining back at me. I visualized a grizzly standing on his hind legs. "Lydia, go up the tree!" She did. Rooted to the spot, I was incapable of turning around and running to the tree. I just continued holding the flashlight on its eyes. After an eternity, it seemed, the eyes moved away and a large set of antlers loomed in the flashlight beam. Moose! A bull moose wanted a drink in the river. Lydia backed down out of the tree and crawled into her sleeping bag. Too wired to sleep, I lit a small fire in front of the tent and sat there all night, keeping the fire going, until dawn.

On our fourth day of hiking, we crossed rough Boulder Pass, still partly covered with snow in late August. It was hard going for Tonka, trying to negotiate a jumbled maze, of what else, boulders, and no trail across. So I let him find his own way. He never hesitated or balked, choosing to stay with us rather than be left. We dropped down to Kintla Lake, where we planned to camp that night, but a large red sign declared that the camps along the river were all closed due to a "grizzly incident," with fresh large-clawed tracks and bear turds conspicuously evident.

This particular part of the trail was through very dense forest - forbidding and scary. I quickly shifted some of the gear, and patient, cooperative Tonka carried us though a mile or two of the spookiest woods, his ears working overtime. In case a grizzly did appear, and Tonka bolted, we preferred to be on board. We soon dismounted, though, because Tonka was packing too much weight. We plodded along the narrow trail in the dark, too tired to worry about anything except putting one foot in front of the other. After an arduous twenty-five mile day-long and part of the night hike, we finally dragged ourselves into the heavily used campground at the foot of Kintla Lake.

Tonka proved to be a great help, and more than that, a good friend.

Kintla Lake
Glacier Park

SUNRISE

June 1973

Every day Blue renewed the bond with his mares. At least once a day and sometimes more, Blue would approach a mare, posture, crest, snort, and stamp the ground, effectively telling this particular mare he adored her, she was his, often nuzzling her on the neck. Each of his mares received elaborate, undivided attention. It only took a couple of minutes, but it was enough to cement the relationship so the mare would not think of going off down the road or across the fields to some other stallion.

One or two mares over the years were indifferent to this display and Blue responded in kind. A few definitely loved it and were as loud as Blue in their squeals

Yuki   *Blue*

and stomps, swishing their full tails suggestively. Yellow Belle needed more than once a day reassurance, demanding and receiving as much attention as she required.

Blue nuzzling Raven

Trouble brewed when Sunrise joined the herd, a pale red dun with blonde mane and tail. This blonde was a home wrecker, upsetting the entire ranch. She would not keep her place in the pecking order, constantly breaking rank, vying for Blue's attention. Pushy, loud, undisciplined. She only lasted a year before I sold her and her foal, Sundown, and peace and harmony were restored to the herd. Sunrise then had a fine life as a riding horse where her strong personality suited her male owner.

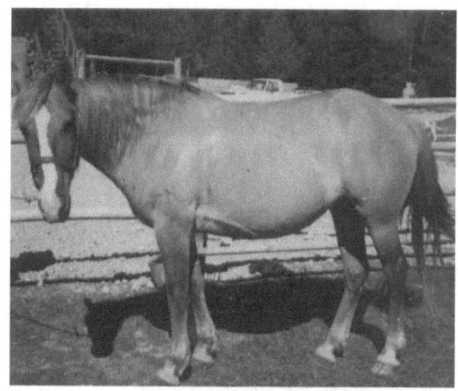
Sunrise

LIO MERCY

August 1973

As a favor to another Montana breeder who was moving away, I agreed to let old Lio Mercy live out her life on my ranch. She was one of the early Spanish Mustang Registry mares, foaled in 1953. She had no training other than haltering, and had never allowed anyone to trim her feet. Her name means "she of little mercy." She arrived early summer, and was turned out with Blue and his herd. Lio had foaled numerous offspring and was showing her age with a perpetual sagging belly.

Lio

The next year in late fall, as the herd walked back from Dudley Slough, Lio refused to come, staying in the woods, and Blue nonchalantly left her there. Unusual, because a stallion always follows behind the herd when going somewhere in order to protect the whole bunch

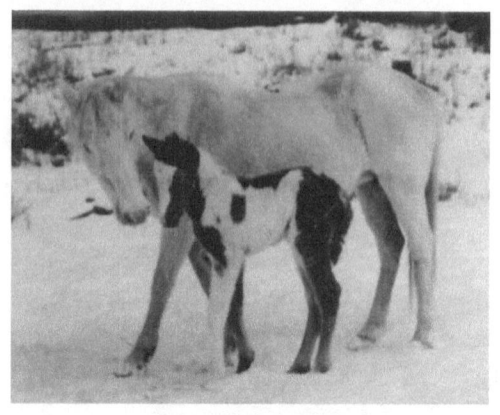 with the lead mare in front. After three weeks of many visits trying to entice her home with oats, she proudly appeared with her new foal. There was snow on the ground, the temperature at zero, but they both looked fine and healthy. Lio allowed me to halter her, and we walked back to the ranch with her beautiful baby.

YELLOW BELLE

May 1974

Yellow Belle, in the middle of the mares and foals
walking the dirt road two miles to summer pasture,
suddenly bolted and ran into the woods with Blue in hot
pursuit. Riding the stallion, I tried to slow him down to
have time to duck under the
branches. He half-reared,
inferring, "Please get off, so
I can catch that mare." I
jumped, snatching the bridle
with me, as it would tangle
in the trees.

Yellow Belle

Yellow Belle, a twelve-year
old pale yellow buckskin
with flecks of gold in her
brown eyes, arrived at the
ranch the prior year. She
was an untrained mare, range bred and reared, who
always resisted any handling. This was Yellow Belle's
first time to Dudley Slough, the herd's summer and fall
pasture. Yana, the head mare, was haltered and in the
lead. Blue and I brought up the rear. Everything was

going well, Yana moving along quickly with her handler when Yellow Belle broke rank. Blue soon caught up to Yellow Belle, stirrups flapping, gave her a good going over for her disobedience, and brought her back to the bunch. She never tried that again.

While on summer pasture with the herd some years later, she was shot in the left shoulder, just below the withers. Did a near-sighted poacher mistake her for an

Blue, Yellow Belle, and foal

elk? Who knows. Enticing the herd into a small corral with oats, I haltered her and we walked back to the ranch. After extensive cleaning and probing, the vet closed her wound leaving a drain tube in place, saying he couldn't find the bullet and did not want to dig around anymore. For three months, I flushed out the wound daily, with her head in a feed trough of hay or oats, until it finally healed. She tolerated my doctoring with great equanimity and restraint.

The following spring, before the herd would be walked to Dudley Slough, Yellow Belle, who was due to foal, was turned into a clean, dry, grassy fenced acre next to the herd's pasture in front of the house. One morning she was standing very close to the far fence. It didn't look right, so I walked out to check, and her new foal was lying down on the other side of the fence. I went through the rail, bent down to shove the foal under the rail when I felt something tug on my hair. Looking up, Yellow Belle's eyes glaring in fury, her teeth bared just inches from my face, ready to bite if I touched her baby! Talking all the while, backing off slightly, I kept my eye on her as I gently and quickly pushed the foal under the bottom rail. Thought she might appreciate what I did for her, but no, Yellow Belle did not ever lose her mistrust of people.

Yellow Belle and grandson

TONKA

June 1974

On a warm day, I rode Tonka to Fortine Creek, where
there was a pool about eight feet deep and twenty feet
wide.   We were entering three long-distance competitive
trail rides (thirty to sixty miles
in length) and I thought it
would be a good idea for him
to have some experience
swimming in case we ever
had to negotiate a strange
river in our travels. He did
not hesitate or slow down
walking across the creek even
though his head gradually

disappeared under the water. With just a halter on him I
could not raise his head. Unperturbed, he continued on
his way and walked up the bank on the other side.

We had better success in the clear water of Dicky Lake,
this time with his bridle on. When the water rose up his
neck, I gently raised his head with the reins, and very
easily he started swimming, making a graceful circle
before heading back to shore.

Trotting downhill on an old, narrow dirt road a few miles from the ranch, Tonka and I rounded a corner and less than a hundred feet away a moose was trotting up the hill very fast on his long flexible legs. If we had ridden just a few seconds faster, Tonka could have climbed the steep rise to our left and we would have been out of the moose's way. With a sharp drop off on our right, a sheer bank on our left and no time to turn around and go back up the road, we were in a bad place at the wrong time. We had about three seconds to contemplate our fate. Would we be forced over the cliff, run over, or kicked?

Suddenly the moose swerved, trotted easily up the slope and disappeared into the trees. Letting out a big sigh, I patted Tonka on his neck for staying calm, and we continued on our ride.

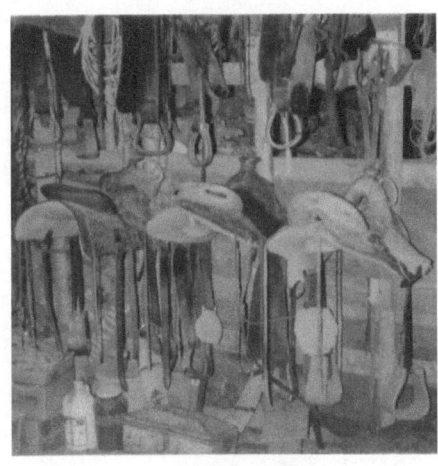

Tack Room

Returning from a long hot training ride, I unsaddled Tonka in the space under the house originally intended as a garage, but never used for that purpose. Shutting the bottom Dutch door, I left Tonka loose in the cool while I stepped into the tack room for his oats. Hearing a funny noise, I turned around and saw the door knob rotating back and forth. Fascinated, I watched, and soon Tonka had succeeded working the door knob enough with his mouth to open the door. He pushed his head through and looked at me as if to say, "What's keeping you so long with my oats?"

Tonka could undo ropes, too. He could not be tied with the usual safety knot that can be pulled free in an emergency. Gates also had to be Tonka-proof. It was a constant game of wits to stay one jump ahead of these intelligent mustangs.

COYOTES

July 1974

Mike

Tonka and I were on a ten mile trot with Mike, my
shepherd collie dog, on a gradual climb to Edna
Mountain, when a large coyote showed himself just
ahead of us yipping in the middle of the narrow dirt
road. He bounded into the trees and about a half mile
later howled at us from a thick cover of brush and trees
as we came abreast of him. Again he pulled the same
trick about another half mile, then tired of the game and
left us. Or was he challenging Mike to follow him?

A few years earlier, two carpenters were working on our new home when Jacques, the only dog with us at that time, followed a coyote who was yipping at him just inside the tree cover. The carpenters said I

Mam and Jacques

would never see Jacques again, but in a little while he came back out from the trees, unscathed.

SUMMER 1977

The chickens had eaten all the grass in their pen, and were let out to scratch around the house. They kept fairly close together between the house and the pen. Having some chores to do, I thought I could leave them for a few minutes. The few minutes stretched into a few more minutes which gave the coyote, who must have been watching, time to pick off one of the chickens. He carried it to the middle of the front acre, and left a few feathers there, along with his droppings. The chickens were shut up in their yard, and never let out again. The next time I left the house, the coyote returned. The remains of a grouse and a few feathers lay neatly in the middle of the acre, along with his droppings. Maybe he was telling me that he did not need my chickens - he could catch his own.

SUMMER 1986

A coyote family with three pups denned nearby. As the pups matured and practiced their calls and songs, one could always be identified by his squeaks. The mother or father would make a low call, and Squeaky would follow, always up in a high register. The parent would try again, with Squeaky in the high decibel range. This went on all summer, Squeaky making very slow progress with his singing, and not sounding like a coyote at all. The family eventually went their own ways, with Squeaky and another coyote, possibly a sibling, staying in the area. I heard him, at the start of winter, making his call at twilight, still squeaky and high, but no mistaking it for anything else but a coyote.

Kwanah

SUMMER 1990

Walking towards the overflow meadow at Loon Lake where the geldings were grazing, I glimpsed a coyote loping into the trees with Kwanah right behind him. As I passed by the twenty five pound salt block put there for the horses, I laughed to see, dead center, the coyote's droppings. No doubt he was getting back at Kwanah for always chasing him off the meadow.

OROENEEKA

June 1975

Oroneeka, Lio Mercy's colorful pinto filly foaled a few days before Christmas, was sold to a buyer in California who would pick her up soon. A Coggins blood test was required for all horses crossing state boundaries.

Oroneeka was walked through the loading chute into the pickup with stock racks and driven to town for the test. Lio Mercy was then turned out with the herd north of the house at the Loon Lake pasture. Coming home, I drove to the Dudley Slough pasture two miles south of the

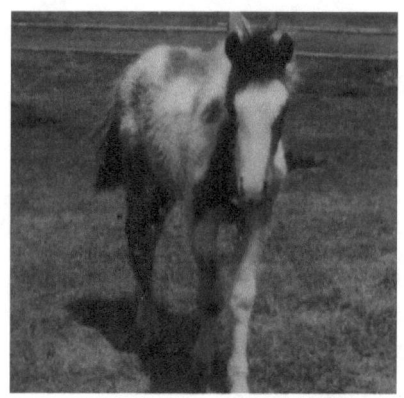

Oroeneeka

house and unloaded Oroneeka where she would have the company of a gelding and a few yearlings while she was being weaned.

The next morning I was astounded to see Oroneeka outside the house, very quiet, very subdued, and very tired. She had gone through the barbed wire fence at

Dudley Slough (tracks in the dirt and tufts of her hair were on the wire), but a careful check of the fence and gates surrounding the ranch revealed no breaks or tracks. Thick woods separate the ranch from Dudley slough. There are no roads on the back side of the pasture where she went through the fence. Oroneeka, never before apart from her dam, had the sense to master two fences and travel two miles through strange woods to find her mother.

TONKA

July 1975

Trotting at a fast clip along the ridge road, Tonka did not require any help from me in pushing or steering, so my mind wandered off in a day dream; not a very smart thing to do in thick woods while sitting on a bareback pad, even though it had stirrups. Rounding a corner, I was startled out of my reverie when Tonka jumped sideways, then bolted ahead in a mad gallop. The

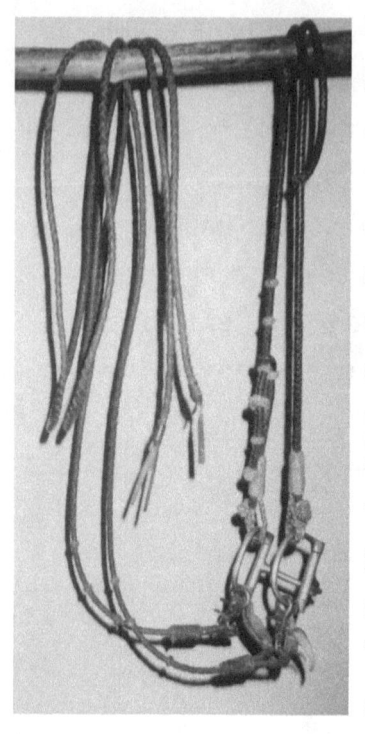

bareback pad slipped, I lost the reins, grabbed onto his mane, and had a strange feeling that I was sitting on his neck. At the same time, a large black bear sow who had been in the middle of the road jumped sideways and ran down the road parallel to Tonka, the two being about ten feet apart. I briefly wondered what would happen if I fell off between the racers, as my seat was terribly insecure. The bear suddenly stopped as all she wanted to do was get back to her cub who was in the grass at the side of the road. But Tonka didn't stop! The wildly flapping stirrups were slapping him in the belly and he ran faster and faster, probably thinking the bear was still after him. After about a half mile or so, I got myself together, let go of the mane with one hand, found the reins, slid back off his neck, and finally stopped Tonka.

On another day, riding the same ridge road, this time with a saddle on Tonka, we came across a bunch of cows spread out on the road grazing on the pine grass scattered among the trees. To avoid spooking them we walked by very slowly, but a large bull started to charge us. Tonka leaped into a fast gallop, going as fast as he could with the bull right behind him. Fortunately, the bull tired before Tonka did, and dropped back.

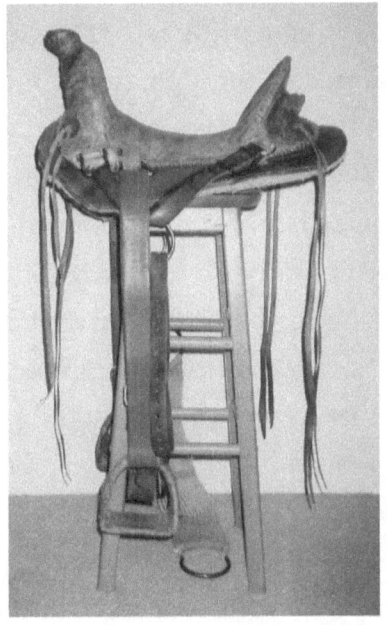

BLUE AND TONKA

May 1976

Every year I rode Blue a little before the herd was turned out on their summer and fall pasture. By the time Blue was nine, with a herd of five mares, he decided he did not want to be taken away from them anymore. Not knowing this, I saddled him up. As I put my foot in the stirrup and lifted my other leg over the saddle, he side stepped away from me before I could sit down. He did the same thing as I tried to mount again. After the third time, I realized that it was a polite way of telling me that if I persisted, it would be a fight. "O.K. Blue, I understand how you feel and I won't ride you anymore." Blue has usually let me know in some way when he is unhappy with a situation, and I have time to change things before he takes charge himself. In this way, the ranch remained peaceful with very few conflicts. It took me a while to understand, and poor Tonka suffered for it.

In training for his second year of long distance riding, Tonka was corralled near the house for his daily, or every other day, ride. Blue and his mares were north of the house on the large Loon Lake pasture with a long walk

downhill from Tonka that should have provided a large enough distance between them. Blue kept his mares at the lake, but every so often he would come back alone and paw the ground in front of Tonka's corral, then return to his mares. He was trying to tell me he did not want Tonka there, but I thought Blue would eventually understand Tonka was no threat to him and his mares. One morning at first light, I heard a commotion and looked out the window.

Blue was inside Tonka's corral chasing him around

Mares at Loon Lake

Blue

and around, sometimes biting at his hind legs. I ran out, and as Tonka came near the gate, opened it enough to let Tonka through, slamming the metal gate in Blue's face. Blue very easily could have smashed the gate open or jumped, but he stayed inside. I ran to the hay barn calling Tonka to follow, and shut him up inside. Then I opened the gate and Blue trotted back to his mares.

Tonka was trailered to Dudley Slough and he had the rest of the year off, to heal his bites.

3 geldings at Dudley Slough

THE BOB MARSHALL WILDERNESS

September 1977

Every September, after the summer's considerable chores are finished, I saddle up Tonka and head for the high country wilderness for one week of trail riding. Surviving the week alone with Tonka gives me the confidence to face another hard Montana winter. Each year I choose a different pass into the Bob Marshall's nine-hundred-fifty thousand acres of rugged mountains, river, and forest which is split down the middle by the Continental Divide. All the summer back packers are gone, and the mule pack strings are just starting to hog the trails to the dude camps for the fall hunting season. No friendly rangers out there to help if needed. They are all in the National Parks. You are on your own.

Tonka and I were on the river trail, high above the Flathead River. First I heard the jingling, then I saw the pack string and one determined horseman in front leading about eight mules tied head to tail, coming at a fast walk. Oh-no! What to do? There was a steep drop-off on my right down to the river, and a high vertical cliff on my left. It was too far and too narrow to back up my horse, and the mule driver was not slowing down. I felt Tonka gather himself up under me. Slowly, he moved one hind leg forward, and then the other one. Next, he moved one front hoof slowly backwards, then the other one, and slowly repeated the whole sequence. When front and back feet were as close together as Tonka could manage, he very slowly and carefully pivoted around, sliding his feet around in one spot. When we were facing the open trail in front of us, he broke into a trot, staying in it until we came to a wide place in the trail and could let the unrelenting pack string go by.

Four years later Matt showed up with his mare to work on the ranch and wanted to see the Chinese Wall, a spectacular fifteen mile long billion year old limestone reef, with a thousand foot sheer face. O.K. we'll go this fall.

We loaded our three Spanish Mustangs into the four-horse stock trailer: Matt's Zulie, Raven, a fourteen year old brood mare that was being packed for the first time, and Kintla, a gelding that I was training. We unloaded four hours later at Beaver Creek, a horse camp and trail-head for many parts of the Bob Marshall Wilderness. Oh, for heavens sake! We left the sawbuck pack saddle back at the ranch. My saddle was a light-weight Western and Matt's a McClellan Army Saddle. The McClellan would make a good pack saddle on Raven with our gear tied on each side. But what would we do for Zulie's saddle? An extra saddle blanket, a scrounged discarded cinch to go under Zulie's belly, the stirrups off Matt's McClellan, the whole thing tied up with baler

Kintla, Raven, and Zulie on trail

twine and there it was, Matt's new saddle. We were off. Every couple of hours Matt and I swapped places, so we both had equal time on the bareback pad; not easy going on the rough, rocky trails.

Chinese Wall

We climbed to the divide, crossed Spotted Bear Pass and Larch Hill pass, marveled at the Chinese Wall, and continued on a loop trail back by way of Bungalo Mountain. Unknown to us, part of the mountain had sloughed off, and an inch of snow covered the steep slope over loose red dirt. A tiny, narrow track spanned the slide area. Matt was in front on Zulie, leading Raven. I was on Kintla behind them. It was too late to turn back. Zulie never broke stride even though Raven was vainly trying to walk on the uphill side. I took one terrifying look at the awful drop into space and tried to sit absolutely still, but must have leaned a little into the mountain, as Kintla compensated by leaning the other way, head and neck over the chasm. Seeing nothing below him did not seem to faze Kintla. After what seemed like an eternity, we reached firm ground, our mustangs' value rising with each steady step.

Kintla

DEEP FREEZE

January 1979

Alone again in January, the coldest month of the year. Hay, oats, and cords of wood were stockpiled. While still warm in bed at 6 a.m. under my electric blanket, I would turn on the lamp to check out the bedroom windows. If there were a few inches of ice buildup inside the windows, it was around 0° outside, if six inches up the glass it was probably minus 10°. At twelve inches it would be minus 25° and a long grind of feeding horses three times a day, chopping ice out of the water tanks that did have electric floating heaters but could still freeze, carrying buckets of warm water to the few horse corrals that did not have water or electricity, and carrying armloads of wood for the two stoves. If the ice was halfway up the windows we would all be in trouble.

The outside thermometer, which was visible from the kitchen window, dipped alarmingly to minus 32°, the next morning to minus 34°, and then to minus 36°. This much cold means clear skies. During the day, the weak sun would gradually warm the temperature up to minus ten and sometimes to zero, before dropping. Early morning, some of the horses' nostrils would be so clogged with ice, they could barely breathe. One or two at a time would be haltered and taken into the garage, which stayed around 10°. As soon as the ice cleared from their noses, out they would go and another group come in.

The heavily pregnant mares due to foal in April were having the hardest time. Even with feeding them all the hay they could eat, plus

Kiote and Kuitan

oats, they shivered in the morning. I drove sixty miles to Kalispell to buy four flannel-lined canvas horse blankets. At last light at 5 p.m., when it was already minus 25°, the blankets would go on. These were just halter trained mares who never had anything on their backs. I had to work slowly and carefully, especially the first time. It was difficult trying to fasten the small metal buckles under the belly without my warm sheepskin mittens which had to be removed because they were too bulky. My fingers, quickly going numb, had to be warmed under my arm pits many times before the four mares were blanketed and buckled. Surprisingly, Yana and Yellow Belle, the most resistant of the mares, accepted the

46

blankets, and to my great relief, still wore them intact in the morning. As the sun warmed up, the blankets came off, otherwise the horses would sweat under them. As

Uno and Quinna

long as a horses' heavy winter coat does not get wet, they stay insulated from the cold. Running my hand under their fur coat to check if they had a good covering of flesh over the rib cage, it was always reassuring to feel their warm body heat.

Unfortunately, the house had some problems. Downstairs is a large garage area that was never used to park any vehicle. The metal garage door was replaced by a single wooden Dutch door. An inside door opens into a tack room, where all the horses' gear is stored, with a work bench, a small wood stove, and a bathroom. Upstairs is a compact kitchen-dining-living area, and a bedroom. At minus 34° the water pipes downstairs froze. Friends Linda and Bill drove fifteen miles to come and thaw them out, and then it was necessary to burn a lot more wood to keep the downstairs warm. But when the three foot section of pipe from the house to the septic tank froze, that was a disaster. The outhouse, built for the house trailer I once lived in, was one hundred fifty feet up the hill which required dressing warmly and trudging through the snow. Since no water could go down any drain in the house, all wash water had to be dumped outside until the April thaw. Gradually it warmed up over the next two weeks to a very tolerable minus ten. Fortunately, we all survived: fifteen horses, two dogs, a cat, the chickens, and a lone snowshoe rabbit in a burrow under the wood pile, its tracks going around the stacked firewood to eat the hay I left out there every night.

Long walk to outhouse

BLUE

July 1979

 Blue can jump or go through any fence on the place if he so chooses, as he has done on a few occasions. Standing next to the fence, he slightly lowers his haunches and gracefully sails over.

This summer, two helpers were building a five foot jack fence across the pasture at Dudley Slough. The mares and foals grazing to the south paid no attention to the work, but Blue would saunter over to watch. When the fence was finished, the workers took a break, sitting on the grass to admire their efforts. Blue walked up to the fence, easily jumped over, casually grazed around for a little while, then jumped back over to his herd.

colt and granddaughter

NAN AND YUCHI

August 1979

Three young horses, one of them mine, found a hole in
the fence and disappeared. For the next two days, I
trailered Tonka sixteen miles to their empty pasture and
rode around looking for them and their tracks. The
whole area is heavily wooded, hilly, and open to range
cattle. Missing were Nantahala (Nan) my two year old
filly, Yuchi a two year old gelding I had sold to Linda a
year ago, and Echo, Linda's small mare. Linda had called
me a few months prior saying Yuchi and Echo were
going to graze the summer on pasture a mile from her

Yuchi and Nan
yearlings

house. Since her daughter would be taking Echo out of the pasture to ride, Linda thought it would be better to have another horse there as company for Yuchi. I trailered Nan up as she and Yuchi had spent their first year together. Echo had never been to the ranch.

Coming home late afternoon of the second day of searching with Tonka, the three horses were on the dirt road just two miles from the ranch, inside my neighbor's large fenced pasture with cattle guards on the road at each end. They must have traveled directly cross country, jumping any fences on their way or walking over the cattle guards with their small hooves on the far end of the guards, on the narrow strip between the grates and the fence. There are no connecting roads from Linda's to Loon Lake Ranch, only the county road.

MONTANA

December 1980

Montana, a feisty three year old grulla stallion, spent the winter in the stud corral, one of many corrals and pastures around the house. It had a ten foot wide metal gate closed with a chain on one end and two hinges bolted into a stout post on the other end. I chose this grulla colt out of the weanling bunch at the Cayuse Ranch in 1977 for his overall good looks and color. He would be bred to some of Blue's fillies to enlarge the gene pool at the ranch.

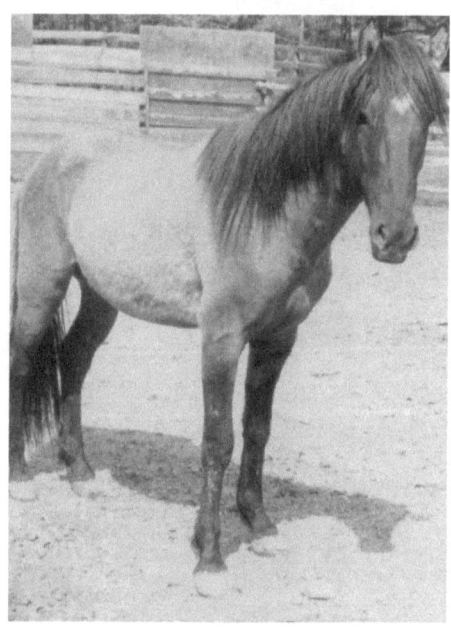

Montana, yearling

Montana was a very inquisitive youngster, testing everything with his agile nose and able to turn and swivel his neck in all kinds of positions.

There had been a brief thaw and all the corrals had

5 years old

chunky ice under the snow. A clanking noise kept waking me up all night, and I thought it might be one of the horses hitting a gate. Looking out the window at dawn, I was startled to see a strange-looking apparition in Montana's corral, and raced out in the gray light. It was Montana standing in the center of his corral with his head and neck through the gate, the weight of the gate bending his head down. The gate had lifted off its hinges and chain closure, and the clanking I heard was Montana trying to back away from the gate. I rather suspect he was embarrassed for any of the horses to see him in his predicament and had backed out of the line of sight of Blue. I eased his head and neck sideways and pushed him out of the gate, then ran, dragging the gate to the opening, tying it in place before Montana could run out yelling a challenge to Blue.

This young whippersnapper could not tolerate another stallion on the ranch. Unlike him, in the winter when all the horses were corralled around the house, Blue tolerated any horse, including mares he was not to breed, geldings, and young colts and fillies, as long as they were all south of his imaginary line, about one hundred feet and he and his mares were north of this line. Blue was happy when this rule was followed, and the ranch ran smoothly. But Montana was something else.

On a lead line, he was a gentleman and did what he was asked. Under saddle he behaved well until we walked out the ranch gate. Rebelling by half-rearing, crow-hopping, balking, whatever was in his bag of tricks that day, he always stopped short of unseating me. After about a mile he finally stopped his shenanigans and we had a peaceful ride. He objected going out the gate because he was probably thinking that one of Blue's mares might separate from the herd and he would miss his chance to run off with her someplace. You never know, it pays to be watchful all the time.

Montana was turned out early in his life with another yearling, a filly, but they were soon parted as he tried to breed her all the time, and I did not want either one to breed yet. Turning him out with the geldings sometimes worked, sometimes not. There was no other available mare for him, and he did not want just one mare. He wanted to be herd stallion and run Blue off the ranch, although Blue and I knew this was not going to happen. In the meantime, I continued with his training, his broken fences were repaired, and he was bred to select mares for two years. At four he was gelded, and at five we rode in the Selway-Bitterroot Wilderness for one week, and he came out of there ready to face the world. Some of his aggressive behavior was re-directed into long distance endurance riding, under his new owner, where he excelled and enjoyed overtaking and passing the other horses in the race.

Montana, May 1990, won the 250 miles (50 miles/day) Pony Express Ride; best time for the entire 250 miles using the same horse.

NAN'S FOAL

May 1983

All the mares had foaled and it was time to take the herd to Dudley Slough. Nan had been the last to foal, but her grulla colt was more than able to keep up with the herd at two and a half weeks old. Because the large pasture at Dudley Slough needed a rest from grazing, the horses were walked to an adjoining wooded pasture. It had a fairly large open meadow, longer than it was wide. What happened next was unusual because Blue always stays

Nan and foal

on the perimeter of his herd watching for danger. Nan's colt was quite precocious, and he reveled in his new-found freedom to run and explore. Not being timid, with a dam who was not at all protective, he was venturing farther and farther from mama. Some foals will not leave their dam's side nor will some mares allow them to run off. Thick woods bordering the meadow, curious foal, unconcerned dam, Blue perhaps dropping his head momentarily to graze, a hungry mountain lion watching and waiting, a lightning fast pounce and it was all over for the foal. Blue charged, the cat dropped his prize, clawing thirty-five feet up the nearest tree, a skinny lodgepole pine ten inches in diameter, pruning it almost to the top, sinking his claws deep in the bark.

Checking on the horses the next day, I found a subdued herd at the edge of the trees, but Nan's foal was missing. A quick look around, and there he lay, at the base of the tree, a broken neck, unclaimed.

RENDEZVOUS PARADE

March 1984

Out in Montana, the town of Eureka,
Mountain men having their March Rendezvous.
Clouds hanging low and a light rain was falling,
The temperature reading a cool thirty-two.

We packed up and saddled four feisty mustangs,
Lined up on Main Street and joined the parade.
Log trucks, loud mufflers, buglers and drummers,
And the black powder blasts of the buckskin brigade.

Wild-eyed and snorting, our mustangs cavorting,
Oh, how they wanted to run.
Starting and stopping, the guns still a'popping,
Our hands cold and clammy, our arms growing numb.

And at long last, we rounded the corner, and smiled at
the judges,
I guess it was worth it, we won the first prize.
Out in Montana, the town of Eureka,
We'll always remember that wild mustang ride.

by Matt Olason,
To the tune of El Paso

Cuervita, Matt on Kintla, Raven,
Phyl on Zulie

Raven and Zulie

Cuervita and Kintla

Phyl on Zulie
Rendezvous Parade, March 1985

Matt on Montana
June 1983

BLUE

June 1984

A Spanish Mustang breeder trailered three of his mares to the barn pasture at Dudley Slough where Blue and his herd were grazing. Blue told his mares to stay put and galloped over to the trailer holding the mares that had

Dudley Slough

never been in a stud band. As the mares were let out of the trailer, Blue took each one in control, herding her to the little bridge over a creek and to the northwest corner of the fenced pasture. His

mares were quietly watching the show about two hundred feet away. One or two of the new mares tried to go her own way, running off. Blue would put on a burst of speed, overtake the mare, and herd her back to the corner. It was necessary for him to do a bit of running to keep the three undisciplined mares in check. After only a few minutes, the three were in the corner, Blue patrolling back and forth, until they got the idea they should stay put. Blue could then take a breather, standing in one spot to rest, a little apart from the three mares, but in a position he could readily keep them corralled. He kept them in a tight bunch until they learned this was the way it would be, which took two days. The three were then allowed to integrate with his mares, who had stayed away until Blue decided they could all be together.

CETAN

November 1984

Late fall, after hunting season, about a foot of snow on the ground, Cetan, son of Montana and Nan, now three and a half, had progressed far enough along in his training to go for a short ride outside the ranch gate.

Matt, on Kintla, would lead, as I thought Cetan would prefer to follow on his first foray into the unknown. But eager Cetan immediately moved out to lead in his fast, long-strided walk.

Cetan, 4 years

We trotted too, but not much. We looped around to the old Ekholtz homestead, and thinking we had gone far enough, decided to take a shortcut over the ridge back to the ranch. Things look differently in the winter, and I could not find the old logging skid trail. Not more than twenty five yards away in a little clearing on the ridge, stood a magnificent white tail buck, with a massive rack, proudly and belligerently proclaiming his territory, his swelled neck telling us he was still in rut and totally without fear. We stopped and admired him, this beautiful, wild creature in his prime that had successfully eluded his predators: man, mountain lion,

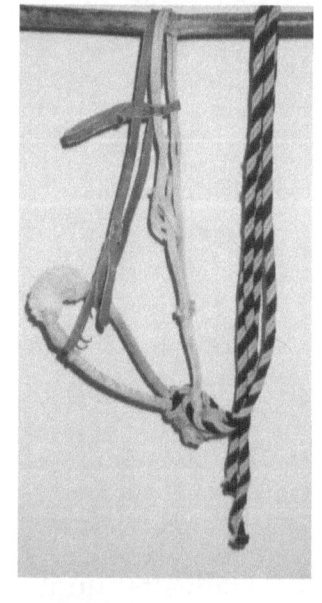

and coyote, for perhaps six or seven years. We wished him well, and quietly left, Cetan ploughing through the snow, breaking trail, finding his way through heavy timber. Some miles later, the "shortcut" having morphed into a cross country ride, Cetan, still eager and strong, led the way home.

Prior to the cross country ride, Cetan and I were on one of our little training rides inside the gate. Walking up to an iced over large puddle in the road, very dark and menacing, Cetan chose to go around it brushing next to

the Douglas Firs lining the road. A large snow-laden branch that he pushed aside swung back and swatted him in the butt. Not knowing what kind of monster was behind him, he took off bucking through the trees. I lost my wool hat and was doing okay until he made a sharp turn, and lost me as he kept going. I picked myself up, wiped the snow off my face, and searched for my glasses. Stumbled home for another pair, got back on Cetan, who was just hanging around the corrals, and went for another uneventful ride.

YANA

April 1985

Blue and Yana

After Yana foaled in early spring, she was kept away from Blue, as I did not want her bred. Every fifth year, brood mares get a rest from foaling, and this had happened twice before with Yana so Blue was not concerned. Nan and Blue were walked over to Dudley Slough, and Yana was turned out with the group pasturing around the lake, north of the house. Needing to reduce the number of my horses, I had written to a Spanish Mustang breeder in North Dakota offering Yana, whose grandsire was an appaloosa, for his appaloosa breeding program. On November seventeenth, he telephoned to say yes, he would like Yana, unbred, and would pick her up as soon as possible.

A few days later, Blue jumped the fence at Dudley Slough, followed the east boundary fence of the ranch to the lake pasture, which he had never done before, crashed through the barbed wire fence, chased off old Tonka and a few young mares, and tried to herd Yana through the downed barbed wire fence. Instead she raced up the hill toward the house. I had just stepped outside and caught a glimpse of Yana and good heavens, Blue, running back and forth along the fence line, Blue every so often mounting her. I opened the gate into the corral behind the house, hollered to Yana, who came running in, Blue hot behind her. After Calming them down with oats, I lured Yana into the stall with more oats where she could be haltered. I then haltered Blue, he being most cooperative, his mission accomplished, and led them back to Dudley Slough. Blue was determined to have Yana, and in the interests of keeping the rest of the fences intact, I let Yana go with him.

Being bred in November, Yana would foal next winter. The coming spring, while all the horses were still corralled around the house, I managed to load Yana in the horse trailer. Blue had been shut in the barn. I let Blue out to see that Yana would be leaving. He made a terrific fuss, bellowing out his objection, but as we drove away, Blue herded Nan to a far corner of his pasture and stayed there with her watching and listening.

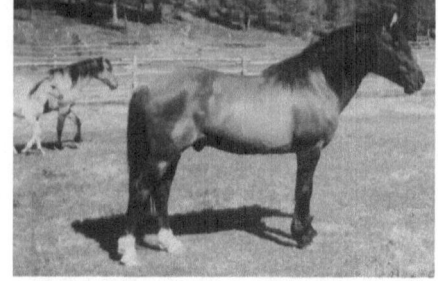

We drove to a friend's place, seventy five miles away, who owned two of my mares, one a daughter of Yana, who would be company for my mare.

Nan and foal   *Blue*

Trece, Yana's thirteenth healthy foal, showed appaloosa markings, same as her dam, and they were both trailered to their new home.

Wind River
Blue x Yana

PALOMINO MARE

June 1985

A well-aimed kick from the palomino mare sent me
flying. It was early morning, in the corral behind the
house, on the far side near the trees. The mare had been
standing next to her motionless foal, and I walked up to
her, quietly talking, to see the newborn. It had been
foaled a little earlier, as her coat was dry, and as I leaned
a bit closer to check for injuries, I realized, painfully, that
was the wrong thing to do. Rather slowly, I walked back
to the house, returning with Matt, a halter, some oats,
and a nursing bottle.

The mare was here to be bred by Blue this summer, as her
owner needed some good genes in his herd to offset his
inbreeding. The palomino had been bred to her own sire,
and this foal was the result. As I held the now haltered
mare, Matt, very carefully, after a few attempts, milked
the colostrum needed by all nursing babies. With her
head held up, the filly was able to swallow the milk. We
stayed with her all morning, holding her head to keep
her from banging it on the ground. I did take time to call
the breeder who told me he never helped foals who
could not make it on their own, and this filly just had the

wrong genes. Nevertheless, we had to do what we could for the foal, and sadly watched her grow weaker and finally, die.

TONKA

March 1986

Since 1984, Matt and I have ridden in the Eureka Rendezvous Parade. Matt has been in many parades, always taking first prize for his authentic buckskins and saddle made by him. Zulie and Kintla have been our reliable parade and saddle horses, but in the fall of 1985, Kintla was trailered to his new owner in Oregon. It did not leave me horseless, but it did leave me without an experienced town horse. Young horses on the ranch were coming along in various stages of training, but none I would want to inflict on a noisy, band tooting, black powder shooting parade. But, oh yes, there was twenty-five year old Tonka, peacefully enjoying his well-earned retirement. For the past eight years, he has only been ridden a few days each summer when the grandchildren come up on vacation. He had been a great saddle horse, used for ranch work, riding in the wilderness, and long distance rides, but never in a parade or town environment. All the rest of the time he has been leisurely grazing away his days. What a shock to his nervous system to be taken suddenly to town and exposed to all the noise and confusion of a parade. He was adjusting fairly well as we took our place among the other riders just behind the high school band. Steady Tonka, keep your cool. Whammo! All the drummers started flailing away. Old Tonka jumped sideways across the street, then started backing up as fast as he could. It took a lot of reassurance for him to line up again. He was wide awake now, going on adrenaline for the entire route, and because I was holding him back from running, prancing all the way, a sure crowd pleaser. For the first

time, Matt took a second place, and I, all decked out in buckskins Matt had made, took a first, mounted on my fiery steed who came out of retirement for one day of glory.

Tonka   Zulie

BLUE

January 1987

Blue and Nan are still pawing for grass in eight inches of snow at Dudley Slough. Every other day, I take them oats using the four wheel drive truck, and check their ribs under a thick winter coat to feel if they are holding their weight. Matt and I rode over one day, Matt holding the horses out of sight of Blue while I gave them their oats. Blue did not seem upset by the two horses being there. The next time over I rode Kangi, a young mare in

Kangi, 5 years

training, and tied her to a tree hidden from Blue. I gave Blue and Nan their oats, walked back to Kangi, untied her, and headed home at a trot. About a quarter mile later, Kangi suddenly leaped into a fast gallop. My right foot, in its big winter boot, flew out of the oversize stirrup, so slick with wet snow, I could not get my foot back in, and I was having trouble trying to slow Kangi down. Sensing something behind us, I turned my head slightly, and good heavens, Blue was right on our tail! Slapping the ends of the reins in his face did not faze him, and not knowing his plans, I bailed off in a hurry, trying to throw myself out of the way of the horses' hooves. Kangi and Blue disappeared around the turn in the road going very fast.

By the time I got home, Kangi was standing at the gate to her corral, and Blue was having a wonderful time snorting up Chaqua, Zulie, and Raven who were in the corral, heads over the fence all a twitter with the masculine attention. With Blue's nose in a pan of oats, it was easy to unsaddle Kangi and lead her through the gate, halter Blue and walk him back to Nan at Dudley Slough. His tracks showed me where, from a standing start, he cleared the top rail of a spread jack fence without touching it - five and a half feet.

The fence at Dudley Slough that Blue jumped

CHA-QUA

April 1987

Pacer

Soon after I acquired Pacer's Babe to breed with Cetan, she was corralled adjacent to Cha-qua. They seemed to like each other, talking and rubbing noses across the fence. In a few days, I opened the gate to see how they would get along. Pacer immediately started kicking, and to protect herself, Cha-qua stayed butt to butt with her, avoiding the kicks. As soon as possible, the two mares were again in separate corrals. Pacer is a powerful mare, and she evidently damaged Cha-qua in some way.

Cha-qua stood in her corral with her head hanging low, not moving. In a few minutes, she lay down and rolled to one side, three times. She got up, assessed herself, lay down again rolling three times to the same side. Again she stood up, thought a bit, then down for

Cha-qua

another three rolls. After this, she shook herself and began grazing, everything right in her world once more.

A couple of months longer of training and riding around inside the ranch fence, Cha-qua was ready to ride out the main gate. She was a bit stubborn, but I did not foresee any problems. Montana, her sire, was sassy and aggressive. Nan, her dam, was gentle as was Cetan, her brother, foaled one year prior to her.

Matt was on Zulie, and Cha-qua would follow her. After going through the gate, she stopped, with no inclination to join her friend, Zulie, and not responding to any aids. A romel, a section of rein with two pieces of leather, about one and a half inches long by a quarter inch wide attached at the end, was tied to the saddle which makes a pop when flicked lightly to reinforce leg pressure. Turning slightly to reach for the romel behind me, there was a split second when I was a little out of balance. That was all Cha-qua needed. She started bucking, stiff legged, arching her back. I stayed seated in the first buck, the second buck I came out of the saddle and hit it hard when she landed, the third buck my feet came out of the stirrups, and almost in slow motion, my body rose skyward. I landed flat on my back, the ground still frozen although all the snow was gone, my upper back squarely on an unforgiving rock. Cha-qua just walked over to the edge of the road and started grazing, while I stayed where I was, unmoving. Matt took the horses home and came back for me in his Bronco.

My upper back stayed numb for days; since it wasn't the lower back, I could walk and sit. Now my own stubbornness cranked in. Wearing a brace, I continued to ride and train horses, but not Cha-qua.

That summer, a breeder from Oregon arrived to take Cetan back to his place as the herd stallion. While at the ranch, he longed saddled Cha-qua in the round training corral, working and pushing her from the ground until she bucked and

Cetan, 6 years, ready to start his life as herd stallion

bucked, while I watched sitting on the fence. She finally figured out that bucking

Cetan, 10 years

Cha-qua bucking

did not get her anywhere, and settled down to become a great saddle horse. She had the same easy, long-strided gait of Montana and

Cetan. I rode her in two endurance rides, into the wilderness, and eventually sold her to an endurance rider who liked her so well, he bought another young mare.

SMOKEY JOE

November 1987

We were off to the post office in Matt's old Bronco. For some unknown reason, Matt had thrown in a couple of halters, and I had picked up the camera along with the outgoing mail. It was a rather dark and drizzly morning, not good for taking pictures, and we had checked on the gelding bunch yesterday, so there was really no need to check again for another day or two. But, I decided to make a pass by their pasture at Dudley Slough anyway, just in case there was enough light for some pictures.

There is a spring-fed small lake in the pasture with a
drainage ditch on the
south end of the lake
going all the way
through the pasture.
There was hardly any
rain this year, as the
spring had dried up,
as well as the ditch,

Dudley Slough Lake and ditch at high water

except about fifty yards extending from the lake, where
the ditch bottom stayed wet. There is a cross fence in the
pasture with five geldings on the north side and two
mares on the ditch side. Apparently the geldings found a
way around the fence jutting into the lake, and raced
across the ditch at the boggy end to join the mares.
Where Smokey Joe happened to cross, closest to the lake,
the bog turned treacherous, trapping him. Only the top
line of his back and neck were out of the watery muck.
He had probably been stuck in there all night, trying to
keep his nose and head out of the mud. It was a cold and
damp forty degrees,
Smokey was shaking
with the cold, and
wouldn't last another
night.

We maneuvered the
Bronco close to the
edge of the bank,

Bronco

76

eased a halter on Smokey, tied a rope to the halter, the rope to a chain that looped around the trailer ball on the back of the Bronco, and shifted to low gear. The chain and rope grew taut, Smokey's neck stretched, the halter straining to come loose under his chin, and then slowly his body came sliding through the ooze. As Smokey's front legs came free, he struggled and helped throw himself on the bank. Tired Smokey was given a breather before the Bronco pulled the rest of him free.

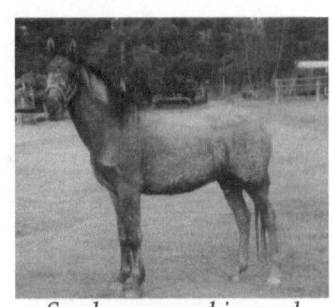

Smokey covered in mud
4 years old

Four year old Smokey had a strong, muscular neck, otherwise this method would not have worked, and different ways would have had to be tried. A shaky mustang tottered to his feet and gamely set out to join the other horses. Since he was covered with thick, wet mud, and trembling with the cold, I walked him slowly home. In a warm barn with plenty of hay and water, a rub down and frequent checks on him, he survived the next critical twenty-four hours. In a few days, Smokey Joe was ready to join his buddies.

2 Years

FIRE ALERT

September 1988

The spring and summer of 1988 was another dry and hot year. Pine beetles attacked the drought distressed pine trees, the orange needles and peeling bark of dead pines were scattered among the still live green trees. The brushy plants and grasses in the forest were crackly underfoot. Streams and lakes were drying up. Add to this, dry lightning storms rumbling and flashing overhead, the threat of a major forest fire erupting was ever present.

One of several lightning strikes caught in the tinder-dry duff in the Dry Fork Creek drainage some miles south of me. The fire was soon running out of control fanned by hot, dry winds from the south, on a direct line towards the ranch with twelve mustangs on pasture and four in corrals. A friend, who had experienced a fire alert two years previously lived seventy-five miles southeast, called to say she could round up a few rigs if necessary.

At 6 p.m. that night I was notified to be prepared for evacuation on a moment's notice. The fire had already scorched thirteen thousand acres, running with the wind through dry timber, moving very fast. The ranch is surrounded by thick woods with only one way  out, to the south. We started gathering up all the horses. The sky was red and the smell of smoke strong. Matt and I walked Blue, two mares and two foals home from Dudley Slough. Next, we hurried down to the lake pasture for the four geldings, two young mares and Matt's horse Zulie. Kangi and Cha-qua were already corralled by the house, plus another breeder's mare who had been bred last summer was in an adjacent corral with her foal. Couldn't we have just turned them loose? No, there were too many barbed wire fences and cattle guards to negotiate if panicked and, a horse might return to its safe home. With all the horses back at the house, I spent the rest of the night trying to decide what to take. Space would be at a premium.

Morning brought more hot winds, red sky, and smoke. My friend, her husband, and their friend showed up at 10 a.m. with a pickup, a four-horse trailer, and a two-horse trailer. Surprisingly, all the horses cooperated and loaded with a minimum of fuss. Maybe they wanted to get out of there, too?

All the tack was piled into the friend's pickup. Pacer and Nan and their foals were in the larger trailer, Kangi and Cha-qua in the smaller; they drove off on a long detour around the fire. At noon, the owner of the corralled mare and foal pulled up with a small open trailer. He wanted a halter and line on the foal to tie him in the trailer next to his mare. Three of us cornered the five month old colt in the barn and with the help of the mare blocking his escape, probably accomplished the fastest haltering ever on an unhandled colt. Pushed him into the trailer for his six hour drive home. Thank goodness for friends with rigs in a crisis.

Three of the younger geldings and a young mare were loaded into my four-horse trailer, some hay bales tossed into the back of the pickup, and we drove twenty miles north to a friend's corral. Unload, back to the ranch. That left Blue, Zulie, old Tonka, a two year old filly, and no more halters. I had kept back two saddles and two bridles. We could make emergency halters out of rope, stay at the ranch as long as possible, ride two horses and pony two horses up the hill north of us on a dirt track, and three more miles down hill to the tiny town of Fortine, and if necessary another fifteen miles to a larger town. The four horses stayed unusually calm and quiet in their corrals.

That night, fortunately, the wind turned around allowing the fire fighters to bulldoze a fire break that held on this side of the fire. After about a week, it was safe enough to start bringing the mustangs home.

SUN RIVER

September 1989

Matt on Kiote, leading Kuitan

We all had an adventure when we rode into the Sun River Game Preserve on the east side of the Rocky Mountains. Matt on Kiote packing Kuitan, and I on Cha-qua rode over Headquarters Pass and down into the beautiful Sun River country, noticing a grizzly on the far slope

Cha-qua

hunting for rodents. We made camp that night near the river, tying the horses securely. A few hours later, a bull elk, bugling loudly, charged through camp heading for the river, probably after another elk infringing on his territory. The horses, agitated and shifting around, soon settled down.

After an easy ride the following day and returning to camp, the three horses grazed their way down toward the river. Matt was holding the lead lines of the two geldings, and I was holding Cha-qua. A nearby elk bugled his loud call, and Kiote and Kuitan, not wanting anymore to do with elk, pulled hard on their lines going in the direction of home. Matt had to let go or swim, something the horses could do but not Matt. Cha-qua tried to follow her buddies; I tied her to the closest

Tree Uprooted by Cha-qua

tree and ran to the river. Matt was able to cross on a downed log and chased after the horses, night closing in fast. The elk bugled again, Cha-qua gave a mighty heave, uprooting the five inch diameter tree, dragging the entire tree about twenty feet before she stopped, hopelessly entangled in the branches. I cut her loose, holding her close, hollering a few times so Matt would know where we were, as it was quite dark. Soon Matt showed up having ridden bareback across the river on Kiote, holding Kuitan. The two horses had not gone far because as mustangs do, they put their heads down to graze whenever they get the chance.

TONKA AND THE COYOTES

November 1989

Old Tonka and the two yearling colts, Kwanah and Piite, were pastured on the hayfield. I happened to look out the window and Tonka was lying down with his head up, resting peacefully with two coyotes taking turns pulling on his tail. Another coyote was about fifteen feet away on one side, and another was standing about the same distance on his other side. I put the binoculars down, worried they were testing him and might soon jump him, and raced out there. Tonka stood up, a little slowly, with no apparent problems and I walked him back to the house, putting him in a corral with a small barn. He whinnied all night for

his two colts, very upset he wasn't watching over his young charges, which has been his job for some years. The next day I walked the two colts back and put the three of them in an acre field near the house with a shelter. Tonka was let out during the day and shut up in the shelter at night. He was content with this arrangement as he could lie down at night, knowing his charges were within sight and hearing, and be with them all day.

Matt Trimming Piite, Quanah watching

BLUE AND AIYANA

July 1991

A beautiful red roan mare, with a lot of white splashes on her coat, was trailered to the ranch for breeding with Blue. She was corralled next to Blue and Kangi who were in the front pasture. She was quiet, just like Nan, no flirting or squealing around a stallion. Kangi and her foal would not come near her, and Blue kept his distance, too. Horses raised in a group become used to the colors of their particular herd, and are suspicious of any coat color that is not familiar.

As time went by, Blue became annoyed at her presence, and when she was near their connecting fence, he would rush at Aiyana, telling her to leave. I then put a halter on Aiyana and walked her into Blue's area. Very hesitantly he approached her and sniffed. Well, alright! She's a mare! I turned her loose and watched as Blue tried to integrate her into his small herd.

Kangi snorted and wanted no part of this strange-looking animal. A stallion has to keep his herd together to protect them. He persistently herded Kangi and the foal, with lowered head, a stallion trait, toward

Blue herding Kanqi and foal

Blue herding to Aiyana

Aiyana who was standing patiently in one spot. Again and again, as Kangi veered away, Blue headed her back, until she finally gave in and accepted the weird-colored mare.

Success!

TONKA

November 1991

Dear old Tonka, my best friend for many years, is now on greener pastures. At thirty years, his arthritic hip was

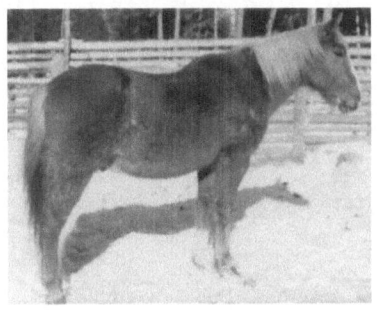

giving him problems lying down and getting up. Was it kinder to let him face another long and cold Montana winter, or let him go peacefully with his nose buried in a bucket of oats?

30 Years

Now that the tears are over, I can think back on our life together with pleasure. Tonka, an eight year old gelding, was my first riding horse, wiser than me in many ways. It took about a year to work out our differences and for

Yuki and Tonka

him to teach me about mustangs. What a thrill it was for this tenderfoot to explore the un-ending woods, going down trail after trail, winding around on old grassed over logging skid roads that often went nowhere. If I got twisted in my directions, Tonka always knew the way home, delighting in choosing the shortest route at a very fast trot. He loved going down new trails as much as I did, and never lost his zest for popping in the pickup or trailer because he knew it meant another new trail to trot. Small, only 13.3 hands, and lightweight, his walk was pokey, his canter rather choppy, but his trot was something else, his preferred gait and mine. He liked the working trot, eight miles per hour and it was effortless to match his rhythm posting or standing in the stirrups. When he shifted into his extended trot, we flew.

Grandchildren

The best thing about Tonka was his willingness to do whatever I asked. We rode fence, helped a neighbor herd cows, competed in three long distance rides finishing in the top ten, and rode into the Bob Marshall Wilderness many times for a week of exploring. In his later years, he carried around the visiting grandchildren. The yearlings and young horses were pastured with him, Tonka teaching them respect and passing on his wisdom.

Watching over his charges

One of my best memories occurred near the end of our long distance training. Our first competition would be at Jackson Hole, Wyoming, riding from seven thousand feet to nine thousand feet elevation. Due to a late snow pack, it was not possible for Tonka to have any high altitude training. About a week before the ride, the passes into the Bob Marshall opened up to give us at least one day in the high country. We headed for Gordon Pass, a nine mile steep and steady climb. At the top, Tonka's reins were tied to the saddle and he could wander at will to graze, while I stretched out flat on the ground. After looking around and seeing nothing edible, Tonka walked back, dropped his head just inches from my belly and closed his eyes for a well-earned nap.

27 Years Old with 3 geldings

BLUE

October 1992

Blue had only one mare now, Kangi, and could only breed her on the day she chose to stand. He could no longer run or trot or even walk fast. We both knew his breeding days were ending. Blue had a wonderful winter two years prior with the first foal, a colt, of the Blue-Kangi cross, Halconer, who would be my future herd sire.

5 Years

Usually foals are weaned at six months by taking them from the herd. Blue would not tolerate yearling colts or fillies in his herd. This is normal behavior in the wild and prevents inbreeding. This year was different. Halconer (Con) was foaled in June, due to be weaned in November. Surprisingly, Kangi weaned Con herself in October. A creep feeder was set up in a corner of the barn, with a small opening for Con who could eat hay in there whenever he was hungry. Kangi and Blue were given hay morning and night in their individual open stalls in the barn.

22 Years

I observed the three horses often, and would remove Con whenever Blue showed signs of intolerance. He never did. All through the long, cold, and snowy months we watched Blue and Con playing. Con would beg Blue to run and they would chase each other until Blue tired or had enough. At times Blue taught Con the ways of a stallion, showing him where to bite and where to grab and hang on to his adversary. He never played too rough or hurt Con. It was beautiful to watch them cantering in large circles in the newly

Halconero, yearling

fallen snow, throwing up clouds of snow flakes behind them. Sometimes even sedate Kangi, although pregnant, would join in.

Come spring, Con was given his own corral within sight of his parents. A good-looking precocious grulla, I was pleased with the cross. Blue and Kangi produced three more foals, all fillies. Blue and

Kanqi and foal, Blue 24 Years

I knew he would no longer be able to breed, and I began thinking of getting an old mare to keep him company. I was physically deteriorating too, and decisions were accelerated when I could barely walk or sit. What I had ignored for years was now shouting at me. In order to heal my long-abused back, it was necessary to leave the ranch.

Often, when Blue, Kangi, and the filly were resting near the house, I would stand next to Blue quietly. What do you want to do? The vet and I talked about alternatives. It was too traumatic on old mares and stallions for spaying or castration. As yet there was no long-term birth control available for mares, and even old mares could come in heat that would create problems for both the mare and stallion. If I kept Blue with me, he would have to be confined in a corral, a mental horror for him. From the time he turned two he had his freedom to come and go on large pastures, always with mares. He could no longer have that freedom because if he went down and could not get up, the ever present predators would close in. What to do? What did Blue want? Gradually in my sessions with Blue, I began to feel very strongly that he wanted to stay where he was. How to accomplish that with the coyotes, mountain lions, and wolves, watching for the weak ones?

Blue was standing peacefully near the house when the vet drove the fifty miles to the ranch, not moving as the vet walked out to talk with him. Very unusual, as Blue was always suspicious and wary of strangers. I was there, ready to hold his halter, but it wasn't necessary. He stayed in the calm and peaceful attitude that he had been in all morning, with no one confining him. After a small dose of tranquilizer, Blue's head drooped, the vet nodded, and I walked Kangi and her filly to the end of the hayfield, through the woods and back to another corral. By the time we got back, Blue was on his final resting place overlooking his pasture. Kangi whinnied a few times, then settled down, content with her foal beside her. She soon left, with her filly, to begin her new life on a Spanish Mustang Ranch in Oregon. All the other horses were sold or given to good homes.

I have a hank of Blue's mane and tail, his memory in my heart, pictures of him on the wall, his genes still going strong in his descendents. He had a good life on Loon Lake Ranch, and it was a privilege to know him. Blue died as I think he would have chosen, on his own turf, with his mare and foal nearby, in dignity and peace.

Daniel Cox

Loon Lake Ranch

Despite its remoteness, the northwestern corner of Montana is becoming increasingly popular for outdoor recreation and second-home development – thanks to its mild (by Montana standards) climate. But the region draws from other species as well. Lying on the northern end of the Salish Mountains – a complex of low rounded hills and valleys - a 520-acre ranch embraces a lake that provides one of the oldest recorded nesting sites sill in use by common loons, a species threatened in the state.

Although almost completely covered with spruce and douglas fir forests, the ranch also hosts a rich variety of habitat types - a marsh, a calcareous meadow, an eight-acre eutrophic pond fed by a permanent spring, and a marl fen (a globally endangered plant community). The wildlife is equally varied. In addition to the loons, great blue herons, ospreys, northern harriers, and red-tailed hawks nest here. Pileated woodpeckers are sighted regularly, and wolverines, mountain lions, bobcats, and moose use the area. The ranch also boasts a rare plant: a substantial population of northern bastard toadflax (*Comandra livida*), considered critically imperiled in the state, occurs in the property's old-growth spruce forest.

Recognizing the potential dangers to her land and wishing to preserve it for wildlife, owner Phyllis Falconer has donated a conservation easement on the area to the Conservancy. Loon Lake Ranch, which is adjacent to the Kootenai National Forest, will be monitored by the Montana/Wyoming Field Office.

in June/July Nature Conservancy News *1986.*